Geronimo Stilton ACADEMY

Grammar Pawbook

1

Text by Geronimo Stilton
Based on the original idea by Elisabetta Dami
Illustrations by Piemme Archives

www.geronimostilton.com

© Atlantyca S.p.A. – via Leopardi 8, 20123 Milano, Italia – foreignrights@atlantyca.it

© 2016 for this Work in English language, Scholastic Education International (Singapore) Private Limited. A division of Scholastic Inc.
SCHOLASTIC and associated logos are trademarks and/or registered trademarks of Scholastic Inc.

Visit our website: www.scholastic.com.sg

First edition 2016

ISBN 978-981-4629-94-2

Welcome to the
Geronimo Stilton
ACADEMY

Well-loved for its humor, fascinating visuals, and fun characters, the best-selling *Geronimo Stilton* series is enjoyed by children in many countries.

Research shows that learners learn better when they are engaged and motivated. The **Geronimo Stilton Academy: Grammar Pawbook** series builds on children's interest in Geronimo Stilton. It makes learning more accessible, and increases learners' motivation to read and strengthen their grammar skills.

The Geronimo Stilton Academy: Grammar Pawbook series comprises three levels:

Pawbook 1 (Junior level)	Pawbook 2 (Senior level)	Pawbook 3 (Master level)
• Explanation of grammar items • Word and sentence level activities • Includes - common and proper nouns - simple sentences - simple present tense - modal verbs	• Explanation of grammar items • Sentence and short text level activities • Includes - subject-verb agreement - the to-infinitive - adjective placement - quantifiers	• Explanation of grammar items • Sentence and text level activities • Includes - indefinite pronouns - gerunds - active and passive voice - complex sentences

Please refer to the contents page for a full list of topics.

Geronimo Stilton titles featured in this Pawbook:

© 2016 Scholastic Education International (S) Pte Ltd ISBN 978-981-4629-94-2

Motivating learners
Authentic excerpts from *Geronimo Stilton* titles interest and encourage learners to read the rest of the story.

Reinforcing grammar skills
The 3-step format in each unit explains grammar items used in context, and provides opportunities for learners to reinforce their grammar skills.

1 **Notes and examples** show grammar items in context, and **side-bar questions** prompt learners to think about their usage.

2 **Simple activities** allow learners' to assess their basic understanding of grammar items.

3 **Sentence and text level activities** help reinforce learners' understanding and usage of grammar items.

Consolidating learning
Each double-page spread consists of an activity related to the preceding units to help consolidate what students have learned.

© 2016 Scholastic Education International (S) Pte Ltd ISBN 978-981-4629-94-2

Contents

© 2016 Scholastic Education International (S) Pte Ltd ISBN 978-981-4629-94-2

1 Terror in the Subway

I dreamed that the subway was chasing me, and that my ears were ringing. When I woke up, I realized it was the phone that was ringing.

"Hello, *Geronimo Stilton* squeaking."

My sister's shriek made me jump. "Geronimooo! Get your tail to the office. **right now!** It's important!" Thea yelled.

I looked at the clock and leaped.

Whaaat? Ten minutes past nine? I was terribly **late**!

"I'm on my way," I told my sister. But I was talking to a dial tone. One thing you should know about my sister. She's not the most patient mouse on the block.

I JUMPED in the shower, brushed my teeth, and got dressed in record time.

Then I rushed to the Singing Stone Plaza subway station.

A **noun** names a person, thing, or place. There are two main types of nouns:

- **common nouns:** these are names for people, animals, places or things, e.g. sister, rodents, office, clock

- **proper nouns:** these are names given to something to make it more specific, e.g. Geronimo, Thea

SINGING STONE PLAZA

Chew on it!

Pick out all the other common nouns in the passage.

Excerpt from *The Phantom of the Subway* (Originally published in Italy by Edizioni Piemme *Il fantasma del metrò*)

© 2016 Scholastic Education International (S) Pte Ltd ISBN 978-981-4629-94-2

Terror in the Subway

I was waiting for my train when I heard a **horrifying** MEOO OOOoHWww!, sound.

The crowd rushed for the stairs, squeaking in terror. "A CAT! There's a CAT in the subway!"

I ran for the exit, too. It was bad enough I was late for work. I wasn't about to become some cat's breakfast sandwich! Rodents were pushing and shoving. I stood back. Oh, yes, I wanted to save my tail. But I didn't want to be crushed to a *FURRY PULP*.

Just then, I noticed an elderly lady holding a young mouse by the paw. "Come on, Grandma," the little mouse cried. But the old lady mouse was frozen with *fear*.

A. Read the text below. Check that the proper nouns are underlined and the common nouns are circled. Cross out the ones that are wrong. Circle or underline the ones that have been missed.

Geronimo Stilton is my uncle and he runs *The Rodent's Gazette*. It is the most popular newspaper here on Mouse Island. When he went to the subway station this morning, he heard a cat meowing. All the rodents pushed and shoved, trying to get to safety. He must have been terrified! Uncle Geronimo is not very brave. In fact, he gets scared easily, but today, he was a hero. He helped save two mice by leading them up the stairs.

B. Which type of nouns are these? In the blanks, write "C" for a common noun and "P" for a proper noun.

1. train _____
2. The Press Club _____
3. Geronimo _____
4. sandwich _____
5. telephone _____
6. Benjamin _____
7. names _____
8. Ratoff Castle _____

© 2016 Scholastic Education International (S) Pte Ltd ISBN 978-981-4629-94-2

Excerpt from *The Phantom of the Subway*
(Originally published in Italy by Edizioni Piemme *Il fantasma del metrò*)

7

Terror in the Subway

What happened when Geronimo reached his office? Complete the text below with suitable nouns from the box. Each noun should only be used once. You do not need to use every noun. Put a cross in the blank if a noun is not needed.

information	Gazette	Thea	motorcycle
door	office	subway	table
Monday	signs	rodents	tiger

Thank goodness I was not late. When I arrived at

the _____, I looked
        1

for _____, my sister.
        2

Suddenly, I heard _____
                          3

the roar of a _____.
                     4

The _____ flew open and there she was.
        5

Even after I reminded her not to ride her bike into my _____,
                                                                    6

she simply giggled _____ and parked it next to my desk!
                          7

She went on and on about the cat in the _____. She even found
                                                    8

out _____ that from _____,
        9   10

rodents had already reported smelling cat pee-pee at Cheese Rind subway station.

In fact, from Tuesday to Friday, many _____ saw
                                              11

_____ of a cat in the subway! Shocking!
        12

Excerpt from *The Phantom of the Subway*
(Originally published in Italy by Edizioni Piemme *Il fantasma del metrò*)

© 2016 Scholastic Education International (S) Pte Ltd ISBN 978-981-4629-94-2

Complete the snippets below with suitable nouns. Use the text on pages 6–7 to help you.

Well, I was waiting for the train at the

_____ when
                               1
I heard a horrifying _____.
                                           2
It was a loud meow! It made my fur stand on end!

Someone shouted that there was a

_____ in
                           3
the _____.
                           4
That just made everyone even more afraid.

… it was utter chaos! Everyone rushed for the

_____. Rodents
                          5
were pushing and shoving one another.

I dashed out like everyone else. I saw a young

_____ holding onto his
                          6
grandma's paw, trying to get her to run, but she was just

too scared. She stood there frozen with fear. Later on,

I heard that some nice mouse helped them and led them

up the _____.
                             7

 Excerpt from *The Phantom of the Subway*
(Originally published in Italy by Edizioni Piemme *Il fantasma del metrò*) **9**

We wanted the scoop on the mysterious happenings in the subway, but it seemed that no one we asked would tell us anything!

Thea twirled her tail. "I just have to know more!" she cried. She picked up the phone and began calling all of her big-shot friends: the mayor of New Mouse City; the chief of police; the city's top cheese inspector; the world's most famouse detective, Hercule Poirat. . . .

She put down the receiver, looking disappointed.

"Rats! This is just **un-be-liev-a-ble!** No one will tell me anything about the subway case!" she complained.

By now, it was already late afternoon.

Suddenly, an idea hit me. "Did I tell you that I've taken up golf again?" I said.

My sister put her paws on her hips. "Geronimo, I'm talking about a huge scoop," she grumbled, "and you're talking about golf. You are so foolish! You are so thick! You are such a cheesehead!"

I rolled my eyes. Why did my sister love to pick on me? …

"For your information, Thea," I said, "I happen to have just met Birdie Whiskers down at the golf club."

My sister raised her eyebrows. I could tell she was impressed.

A **pronoun** takes the place of a **noun**. A pronoun can be the **subject** or **object** of the sentence, e.g.

Thea twirled **her tail**. **She** twirled **it**.

Note:
The **subject** of a sentence carries out the action. The **object** of a sentence receives the action.

In the example above, "Thea" is replaced by the pronoun "She", and "her tail" is replaced by the pronoun "it".

Subject pronouns	Object pronouns
I	me
you	you
he	him
she	her
it	it
we	us
they	them

Excerpt from *The Phantom of the Subway*
(Originally published in Italy by Edizioni Piemme *Il fantasma del metrò*)

© 2016 Scholastic Education International (S) Pte Ltd ISBN 978-981-4629-94-2

Anyone for  Golf?

That's because Birdie Whiskers was always in the news. He was a *championship golfer*. And besides winning tournaments, he also was the head of the entire subway system.

I picked up the phone and called Birdie. I congratulated him on his latest game. Then I asked him about the mystery in the subway. Unfortunately, not even Birdie could talk to me. The investigation was .

I hung up with a deep sigh.

Suddenly, my cousin Trap barreled through the door. Of course, he didn't bother to knock. I don't think he even knows how.

 **Chew on it!**

Which pronoun would you use to replace "The investigation"?

Circle the pronoun in each pair of sentences below.

1. Thea raced to her computer. She found some information about the case.

2. The rodents had been seeing signs of a cat for a whole week! They had seen a shadow of a cat at Curlyfur Court station.

3. Then, Thea and Geronimo had a fax come in. They learned that Inspector Clue Rat was closing the subway!

4. Thea called all her big-shot friends. She wanted the latest scoop.

5. Geronimo had an idea. He would call Birdie Whiskers to find out what was going on.

6. Unfortunately for Geronimo, Birdie refused to say anything about the investigation. Birdie said that it was top-secret.

7. Maybe Trap knew something. He is known for being a pushy mouse!

Anyone for 🏌 Golf?

Complete the text below with the correct pronouns.

Thea called Hercule Poirat, the famouse detective. _____

1

wanted to get some information from _____.

2

However, Hercule would not say anything about the case.

Then Geronimo decided to use his contact. After all, _____

3

did play golf with Birdie Whiskers, head of the subway system. Geronimo asked

_____ about the mystery, but Birdie also could not say anything

4

about the case.

When Trap arrived, _____ announced his plans.

5

" _____ am going to open my

6

own bagel place. I'm going to call it Big Belly Bagels!"

Thea and Geronimo were too busy to bother with Trap. " _____

7

are working on a story about the phantom in the subway!" said Geronimo.

"Can _____ please go away? Leave _____

8   9

to do our work!"

Trap said, " _____ can handle this!" He made

10

some calls and got some information. However, Trap threatened to

sell the information to Sally Ratmousen, Geronimo's archrival. This

made Thea mad, and _____ started screaming at Trap. Before

11

long, _____ were both yelling at each other.

12

 Excerpt from *The Phantom of the Subway*
(Originally published in Italy by Edizioni Piemme *Il fantasma del metrò*)   © 2016 Scholastic Education International (S) Pte Ltd ISBN 978-981-4629-94-2

A. **Read each set of sentences. Underline the subject pronouns and circle the object pronouns. Draw arrows to show what the object pronouns replace.**

1. Trap wanted money for the information.

   He threatened to sell it to Sally Ratmousen.

2. Trap knew that Sally is Geronimo's archrival.

   He tried to persuade her to pay for the latest scoop.

3. Thea and Geronimo were really angry with Trap.

   They could not believe they were related to him.

B. **Read the conversation below. Who does each of the underlined pronouns refer to? Write your answers in the blanks.**

I could use some money for my business. _____

I think Sally would pay me well for the scoop! _____

Are you crazy? _____

You know Sally is my number-one enemy! _____

Yes, but I also know that you will make lots of _____

money on this special edition. I only want 80 percent

of the profits. If you weren't such a penny-pincher,

you would have your story. You're lucky I'm giving _____

you any info at all! _____

I can't believe we are even related! _____

Give us the information now, Trap! _____

© 2016 Scholastic Education International (S) Pte Ltd ISBN 978-981-4629-94-2

3 It's a Deal!

We needed to find out what was going on in the subway, but Trap refused to tell us what he knew. While we were arguing, Pinky Pick heard everything!

Pinky PICK

Pinky hopped up and down on her pink platform shoes. "Everyone **freeze**!" she ordered.

Thea stopped yelling at Trap. Trap stopped yelling at Thea. I stopped chewing my **whiskers**. All eyes turned to my assistant editor.

Pinky is only a teenager, but she is not shy. In fact, she is the exact OPPOSITE. When that mouse starts squeaking, look out. She can talk the fur off a long-haired hamster!

"OK, here's the deal," she began.

1. *Trap tells us everything he knows.*
2. *I tell you how to get by the police barricades in the subway.*
3. *Thea organizes the whole expedition.*
4. *And, Boss, you put up the dough.*

She grinned and went on. "We'll divide the money among all four of us. That's **25** percent for everyone," she finished.

Verbs tell us what is happening.

- **Action verbs** tell how people do things, e.g. hopped

- **Saying verbs** tell how people say things, e.g. groaned

- **Mental verbs** tell how people think or feel, e.g. like

- **Sensing verbs** describe how people use their senses, e.g. smell

Excerpt from *The Phantom of the Subway* (Originally published in Italy by Edizioni Piemme *Il fantasma del metrò*)

© 2016 Scholastic Education International (S) Pte Ltd   ISBN 978-981-4629-94-2

Trap groaned. "What? Equal shares?" he complained. "That doesn't sound fair."

Pinky twirled her tail. "Take it or leave it," she squeaked cheerfully.

For a moment, no one said a word. It was so quiet, you could have heard a sliver of Parmesan drop.

Then Trap stuck out his paw. "It's a deal!" he told Pinky. They shook paws.

Chew on it!

Can you identify all the other action verbs and saying verbs in the passage?

Circle the verb(s) in each sentence.

1. Pinky Pick heard everything.

2. She marched into the room.

3. She ordered everyone to freeze.

4. They all turned to look at her.

5. She told them about her idea.

6. She suggested that they share the money equally.

7. Only Trap complained about that.

8. No one else said a thing.

9. Pinky felt confident.

10. In the end, Trap agreed to the deal.

© 2016 Scholastic Education International (S) Pte Ltd ISBN 978-981-4629-94-2

Excerpt from *The Phantom of the Subway*
(Originally published in Italy by Edizioni Piemme *Il fantasma del metró*) **15**

Trap wrote a list of the information he got. Complete the list below with suitable words from the box.

ask	made	examine	find
gives	says	tell	think

1. Commuters _____ about some cat scratches near the cheese-pop vending machine at Scurryhill station.

2. The crimerat experts are called in.

   They _____ the scratches.

   They _____ that the cuts were

   made by a big cat.

3. They also _____ some tufts of fur and

   a ten-foot-long cat whisker at Cheese Rind station.

4. A catology expert _____ his opinion

   that the dark grey feline could be a giant *Colossal Catitus*.

5. A feline psychology professor _____ a trap for

   the cat a while ago. The trap is made up of a gigantic cage and

   four hundred boxes of Kitty Krunchies.

Excerpt from *The Phantom of the Subway*
(Originally published in Italy by Edizioni Piemme *Il fantasma del metrò*)

© 2016 Scholastic Education International (S) Pte Ltd ISBN 978-981-4629-94-2

A. **Pinky wrote out a plan. Complete the task descriptions with suitable verbs. Use the text on pages 14–15 to help you.**

THE PLAN!

1. Trap must _____ us everything he

   _____ .

2. I will _____ a way past the

   police barricades in the subway. In fact,

   I _____ who I can

   ask to help us! My friend, Goofsnout P. Goofus,

   can _____ a copy of the

   subway map for me. He is the assistant to

   New Mouse City's sewer control manager.

3. Thea will _____ the whole

   thing. She will _____

   the things we need, such as wet suits, rubber

   boots, and flashlights.

4. Geronimo will _____ for all our expenses.

B. **If you could be part of their team, what do you think you could do to help? List two things you could do.**

1. _____

2. _____

Excerpt from *The Phantom of the Subway*
(Originally published in Italy by Edizioni Piemme *Il fantasma del metrò*)

Like a Sewer Rat

A. **Read the text below. Complete it with suitable pronouns. Then circle the nouns that the pronouns refer to. Draw arrows from the pronouns to the nouns.**

Pinky, Geronimo, Trap, and Thea put on the outfits that Thea had gotten them and headed out at eight o'clock. Pinky took _____ to a narrow alley at the
₁
back of the fish market.

_____ showed them a drain and a map of
₂
the sewer system.

"The police have closed all the entrances. The only way to get past _____
₃
is to go through the drain," said Pinky. Trap was impressed with Pinky.

He asked, "How did _____ get the map?" Pinky said that her
₄
friend, Goofsnout P. Goofus, made a copy of _____ for her.
₅
_____ was the assistant to New Mouse City's sewer control manager.
₆

Geronimo refused to go into the sewer. He exclaimed,
"_____ am not a sewer rat! I am a
₇
respectable mouse!" Trap started to tease Geronimo. He
called _____ a 'fraidy mouse and a wimp.
₈
_____ both started to argue, and Thea
₉
had to stop them. "Shhhhh!" _____
₁₀
squeaked. "Shut your snouts and get going!"

Excerpt from *The Phantom of the Subway*
(Originally published in Italy by Edizioni Piemme *Il fantasma del metrò*)

© 2016 Scholastic Education International (S) Pte Ltd ISBN 978-981-4629-94-2

B. **Complete the instructions with the correct verbs. Use the given letters to help you.**

1. R __ m __ __ __ the grating so that you can go down into the sewer.

2. C __ __ __ b down the ladder. Be careful as it might be slippery.

3. W __ __ k along the canal. Sewage should be flowing on your left.

4. When you r __ __ __ h the end of the sewer pipe, c __ __ __ s the number 7 line. You might want to t h __ __ __ a rope across the canal so that you can h __ __ g on to it as you cross over.

5. M __ k __ your way along the number 7 line till you reach Singing Stone Plaza. Remember to s __ __ y clear of the rails.

C. **Someone else had gotten news of the phantom cat. Look at the letters in the green boxes. They will help you figure out who that person is.**

Hint: She is someone Geronimo does not like!

__ A __ __ __   __ __ __ __ __ U __ __ __

Excerpt from *The Phantom of the Subway* (Originally published in Italy by Edizioni Piemme *Il fantasma del metrò*)

4 A Voyage on the Amazon River

My friend, Professor von Volt, invited us to the Amazon. He was searching for an ancient Incan temple that housed a giant ruby. We were thrilled to join him on his journey.

What an UNBELIEVABLE sight! The plants were lush and incredibly **green**. Multicolored birds sat on the branches of the trees. Crocodiles floated like killer logs in the water. Enormouse hairy spiders, carnivorous ants, and poisonous snakes watched us from the shore. I shivered. I was glad I was on the sub. Don't get me wrong, I like WILDLIFE as much as the next rodent. But this wildlife was a little TOO wild, if you know what I mean.

I chewed my whiskers to keep from shrieking with fear. I didn't want anyone to call me a scaredy mouse. I forced myself to listen to the professor. He was giving Benjamin a history lesson.

"The first rodent to land in the Americas was Christopher Columouse in 1492. But he thought he had reached INDIA. That's why he called the local people Indians. After Columouse, the conquistadors arrived from Spain. They were soldiers who conquered land in the name of the king of Spain. Next, ADVENTURERS from Portugal came. They colonized Brazil," he explained.

An **adjective** is a descriptive word that tells us more about a noun. We can place adjectives:

- before nouns, e.g. **carnivorous** ants, a **history** lesson, etc.

- after "is", "are", "was", "were" in sentences, e.g. "I was **glad**." The word "glad" tells us how Geronimo felt.

Chew on it!

What are the other adjectives in the passage used to describe the plants and animals in the Amazon?

Excerpt from *The Temple of the Ruby of Fire*
(Originally published in Italy by Edizioni Piemme il tempio del rubino di fuoco)

A. **Geronimo, Thea, Trap, Benjamin, and Professor von Volt finally reached the beginning of the Amazon River. Read the text below, and circle the adjectives.**

We begin our search for the temple with the professor leading the way. I was tired and sweaty. I couldn't wait to get back home. I felt like I needed a day at a relaxing spa to rest my aching back and blistered feet.

Finally, we reached a tiny village. The villagers were warm and friendly. The chief, Strongfur, greeted us together with his wife and daughter. They were simple mice that lived in the forest, and were respectful of nature.

When we said we were looking for *THE TEMPLE OF THE RUBY OF FIRE*, Strongfur had a strange look on his face. "There is no temple. There is no ruby," he said. "You must give up your search!" Everyone in the village repeated the same thing.

We were shocked, but we thought it best not to argue. For once, even my obnoxious cousin kept his snout shut.

B. **When Geronimo went to explore the surrounding area, he came across some fish in the Amazon. Look at the picture below. Describe Geronimo and the fish with the list of adjectives given.**

small	frightened	colorful
scary	nervous	shocked

© 2016 Scholastic Education International (S) Pte Ltd ISBN 978-981-4629-94-2

Excerpt from *The Temple of the Ruby of Fire*
(Originally published in Italy by Edizioni Piemme Il tempio del rubino di fuoco)

21

 Circle the correct adjectives in the sentences below.

1. The chief's daughter, Monkeyfur, warned me of the (ferocious / ferocity) Biters.

2. At first, I did not know what she was talking about, but later, when I saw the (sharpened / sharp) teeth of the fish, I realized they were piranhas!

3. After my lucky escape, I decided to stop and rest under a (shade / shady) tree.

4. Before I could sit down however, Monkeyfur let out a cry again. I jumped up just in time to avoid the (enormous / enormity) crocodile that was snapping its jaws.

5. Then she pointed out other things that I did not see — a (poison / poisonous) black scorpion hidden in the leaves.

6. Next, she also showed me the (long / length) anaconda slithering on a branch over my head.

7. I was really (impressed / impression) with Monkeyfur. She had saved my life.

8. To thank her, I offered to teach her to read and write. I was really (surprised / surprise) to learn that no one in the village could read or write.

Excerpt from *The Temple of the Ruby of Fire*
(Originally published in Italy by Edizioni Piemme *Il tempio del rubino di fuoco*)

© 2016 Scholastic Education International (S) Pte Ltd ISBN 978-981-4629-94-2

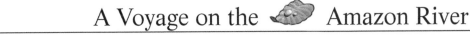
 That night, Geronimo was awakened by a strange sound. Together with the others, he went to investigate. They discovered a team of rodents felling the trees! Write short descriptions of each rodent using all the given words and phrases.

1.

chubby	slick black fur
huge gold medal	thick gold watch
nasty	glittering diamond

This rodent _____

_____

_____

_____

2.

thin	black shirt
crooked snout	evil expression

This rodent _____

_____

_____

_____

3.

fierce	muscular
strong	thick brown fur
enormous	

This rodent _____

_____

_____

_____

© 2016 Scholastic Education International (S) Pte Ltd   ISBN 978-981-4629-94-2

Excerpt from *The Temple of the Ruby of Fire*
(Originally published in Italy by Edizioni Piemme *Il tempio del rubino di fuoco*)

5 The Strangers are Right!

We finally found out the problem the villagers faced — there were rodents destroying their forest!

The next morning, I talked to Strongfur. "We know about the evil rodents who are destroying your forest," I said. "We want to help. We must stop them before it's too late."

Strongfur shook his head sadly. "I'm afraid no one can help," he said with a sigh. "They have threatened to BURN down our homes."

Suddenly, Monkeyfur jumped to her paws. "The strangers are right!" she cried. "We must return to the **HOUSE OF THE HOWLING SPIRITS**, where the tombs of our ancestors are buried!" …

Slowly, Strongfur let us in on their secret. It seems they were the last descendants of the Incas. For years, they had been living deep in the forest next to the House of the Howling Spirits. It was the same as the place we called the *TEMPLE OF THE RUBY OF FIRE*. Then the EVIL RODENTS had come and began chopping down trees. Strongfur and the rest of the villagers were driven away.

I watched Monkeyfur listening to her father. She looked angry. "Father, please let me go with the strangers," she pleaded. "Together we will stop the evil ones. We should not have to live in fear."

After a few minutes, Strongfur nodded. He hugged his daughter. "You may go," he agreed. *"But remember, you must be sly like a monkey."*

The **indefinite articles** "a" and "an" are used to talk about any singular person, animal, or thing. We use:

- "a" before words that start with a consonant, e.g. **a** rodent
- "an" before words that start with a vowel sound, e.g. **an** evil rodent

The **definite article** "the" is used to talk about **specific** singular or plural nouns, e.g. "**the** last descendants of **the** Incas"; "chopping down trees" (no article is needed before "trees" as it is not referring to specific trees).

Chew on it!

Why does Strongfur say "sly like a monkey" and not "the monkey"?

Excerpt from *The Temple of the Ruby of Fire*
(Originally published in Italy by Edizioni Piemme Il tempio del rubino di fuoco)

A.   Circle the indefinite articles in the text below.

We decided to leave for the House of the Howling Spirits. Monkeyfur was our guide. She led us into the forest.

As we walked, I noticed many things. In fact, I was getting to be a good observer! I looked around. I saw things I had never noticed before. I saw an insect hidden in a flower. I saw a snake underneath a mossy tree trunk. I saw a caiman sunk into the mud.

B.   Can you see some of the other things Geronimo saw? Fill in the blanks with "a" or "an". Then circle the animals or insects he saw.

1. Geronimo saw _____ jaguar. Can you find it?

2. He noticed _____ praying mantis on _____ leaf. Where is it?

3. There is _____ anaconda slithering down. Can you see it?

C.   Circle all the definite articles.

As we walked further, we heard a loud sound, like a scream. Monkeyfur told us to be quiet. "That is the scream of the howling spirits," she said.

I was terrified! I hoped that we would not meet any howling spirits. I pulled out my binoculars. I could see Nastytail's campsite, as well as a stone structure covered with vines. It was the remains of the ancient Incan village!

Excerpt from *The Temple of the Ruby of Fire*
(Originally published in Italy by Edizioni Piemme *Il tempio del rubino di fuoco*)

A. **Fill in the blanks with "a", "an", or "the". Put a cross in the blanks that do not need an article.**

1. We saw _____ stone structure covered by vegetation.

2. It was _____ Temple of _____ Red Ruby.

3. It was shaped like _____ pyramid that was missing _____ point at the top.

4. We crept closer to _____ campsite where Nastytail's team was.

5. We saw many _____ trucks there. _____ trucks were filled with _____ logs.

6. Then we heard Nastytail talking. "We will cut down all _____ trees surrounding _____ temple. Those trees are valuable. Soon we will be rolling in _____ cheese," said Nastytail.

7. Bones asked, "What about _____ natives, Boss? What will they do?"

8. Nastytail simply let out _____ evil laugh.

Excerpt from *The Temple of the Ruby of Fire*
(Originally published in Italy by Edizioni Piemme *Il tempio del rubino di fuoco*)

© 2016 Scholastic Education International (S) Pte Ltd ISBN 978-981-4629-94-2

A. **Correct the errors in the sentences below. Then number the sentences (1 to 8) to show the correct order.**

_____ Monkeyfur led the way inside. A light from the flickering candles cast eerie shadows all around.

_____ Monkeyfur showed us the sacrificial altar, and drawings of many different animals and the plants. Then she pointed out a location of the ruby! It was right in the center.

_____ "Do not worry. The screams are from a Howling Spirits," Monkeyfur explained.

_____ We waited for a hour, till after Nastytail and his crew were sound asleep.

_____ Just as I thought I would pass out, I saw an whole bunch of monkeys coming to greet Monkeyfur.

_____ She spoke to them in an strange language before showing us the main room.

_____ All of a sudden, we heard bloodcurdling scream.

_____ Then we headed for a Temple of the Ruby of Fire.

B. **Circle where the ruby was in the picture below. Use the text above to help you.**

© 2016 Scholastic Education International (S) Pte Ltd ISBN 978-981-4629-94-2

Excerpt from *The Temple of the Ruby of Fire* (Originally published in Italy by Edizioni Piemme *Il tempio del rubino di fuoco*)

6 Paws Up!

Monkeyfur showed us where the ruby was and we realized that the place also had a source of oil! Just then, something terrible happened.

Just then, I heard a noise. "Paws up!" a voice squeaked.

We turned around. It was Nastytail and his crew. Fortunately, they had not seen the oil gushing out of the well.

"Hey, Boss. That's Strongfur's daughter," Bones told Nastytail. "Let's hold her hostage. That will make her father obey us!"

Nastytail nodded. "Good idea," he muttered. *"I was just going to say that."*

Miceson stared at us with a menacing look. "Who do you want me to SQUASH, Boss?" he sneered. "Just give me the word and I'll do it!" …

My cousin rolled his eyes. "What a bunch of nitwits," he scoffed. "You haven't even noticed the ruby."

Thea elbowed him to keep quiet.

But Bones perked up his ears. "Yes, legend has it that there's a giant ruby hidden here," he grinned. "We have to make them spill the beans, Boss."

Nastytail nodded. "Um, right. Spill the beans," he muttered. *"I was just going to say that."*

Miceson puffed up his chest. "**Do what the boss said. Spill the bean-sprouts or I will squash you!**" he growled. …

When we want to show who something belongs to, we can use **possessive determiners** or **possessive pronouns**.

We use **possessive determiners** such as "my", "your", "our", "his", "her", "their" before nouns to show ownership, e.g. That will make **her** father obey us.; The ruby was right under **our** snouts.

We use **possessive pronouns** like "mine", "yours", "his", "hers", "ours", 'theirs' in place of a noun, e.g. Miceson puffed up his chest. Look at that chest of **his**!; The ruby is **ours**!

Excerpt from *The Temple of the Ruby of Fire*
(Originally published in Italy by Edizioni Piemme Il tempio del rubino di fuoco)

© 2016 Scholastic Education International (S) Pte Ltd   ISBN 978-981-4629-94-2

Bones giggled. The rest of us kept quiet. The ruby was right under our snouts. But there was no way we were going to tell these bozos.

Bones thought for a moment. "Let's threaten to mousenap Monkeyfur," he said to Nastytail. "That will get them squeaking." …

They grabbed Monkeyfur.

At that moment, the professor jumped up. "Leave her alone!" he commanded. "The ruby is here. Right under your SNOUTS."

He pointed to the well.

The rotten rodents stared at the glittering stone. Three pairs of eyes opened wide. Three jaws hit the ground. "Jackpot!" they shrieked with glee.

Chew on it!

Who was the professor talking about when he said "your snouts"?

 A. Underline the possessive determiners in the sentences below.

1. The natives were forced to give up most of their traditions.

2. Monkeyfur told us about their most prized possession — the oil they got from the oil well.

3. If Nastytail and his gang found out about the oil, they would exploit it.

4. We kept quiet so they would not notice the ruby that was lying right under our snouts.

5. Unfortunately, Bones heard Trap whispering about the ruby, and his ears perked up.

B. Underline the possessive pronouns in the text below.

"The ruby is not theirs; it is ours. We cannot let them get their hands on it. We will fight them and take back what is ours. The decision to stay and help us is yours," said Monkeyfur.

© 2016 Scholastic Education International (S) Pte Ltd ISBN 978-981-4629-94-2

Excerpt from *The Temple of the Ruby of Fire*
(Originally published in Italy by Edizioni Piemme *Il tempio del rubino di fuoco*)

Read the interview below. Circle the correct word to use.

1. Q: Whom did the oil in the well belong to?

    A: It belonged to the Incas, (our / ours) ancestors.

2. Q: Whose monkeys are these?

    A: They are (our / ours).

3. Q: How do you communicate

    with them?

    A: (My / mine) father taught me

    the art of communicating

    with the monkeys.

4. Q: So, does your tribe use the oil from the oil well?

    A: Yes, but we are careful. You should take only enough for (your / yours) needs,

    otherwise there will be nothing left for the future. The resources are not

    (your / yours) alone; they belong to everyone in the world.

5. Q: What are some of the things we can do?

    A: There is plenty you can do. You could reduce (your / yours) water usage.

    You could make sure you recycle (your / yours) used materials.

6. Q: What are some of the problems that you face now?

    A: Many evil rodents want to take (our / ours) trees and (our / ours) resources for

    (their / theirs) own use. Rodents like Nastytail and (his / he) gang are just one

    example of the rodents who try to steal from nature.

Excerpt from *The Temple of the Ruby of Fire*
(Originally published in Italy by Edizioni Piemme *Il tempio del rubino di fuoco*)

© 2016 Scholastic Education International (S) Pte Ltd ISBN 978-981-4629-94-2

 Complete the story with suitable possessive determiners and pronouns.

When Nastytail and his gang first found the group, they wanted to prevent anyone

from stopping their operations. Of course, Trap had to open that big mouth of

_____ and let slip about the ruby!
1

 When they discovered the ruby sitting right underneath

_____ snouts, they were over the moon.
2

Nastytail wondered what the ruby was worth. Bones took

out _____ calculator. They were going to
3

be rich! Just then, a few drops of oil trickled out from the faucet. They

realized that they had found oil as well! "We are going to be rich! All

these riches are _____!"shouted Bones and Miceson.
4

Just as they were thinking of _____ riches, Monkeyfur sent a signal
5

to _____ monkeys. In a flash, they sprang down and hit the villains
6

with stones and leftover avocados. Within minutes, Nastytail and _____
7

sidekicks were begging for mercy. "We give up! You can have _____
8

ruby back!" They were sobbing like babies.

© 2016 Scholastic Education International (S) Pte Ltd ISBN 978-981-4629-94-2

Excerpt from *The Temple of the Ruby of Fire*
(Originally published in Italy by Edizioni Piemme *Il tempio del rubino di fuoco*)

The Amazon Forest

Complete the passage with suitable adjectives, articles, possessive determiners, or possessive pronouns.

What is the Amazon?

It is a region around the Amazon River. It covers a very

l___ ___ ___ ___ (*adjective*) area: more than two million square
     1

miles. The forest there is very d___ ___ ___ ___ (*adjective*),
             2

with a wide variety of trees. It is a rainforest, so it gets a lot of rain.

It is very h___ ___ (*adjective*) there, with temperatures between
     3

77 and 95 degrees Fahrenheit all year round.

Crocodilia

Amazon River

South America

Who lives in the Amazon?

T___ ___ (*article*) Yanomami live in the Amazon. They grow
  4

many different fruits and vegetables. Many of ___ ___ ___ (*article*)
           5

men and women know how to use bows and arrows as they

depend on hunting and agriculture for ___ ___ ___ ___ ___
               6

(*possessive determiner*) survival. The Yanomami are also

very g___ ___ ___ (*adjective*) and skillful fishermen.
     7

___ ___ ___ ___ ___ (*possessive determiner*) huts are made
    8

out of leaves, and they sleep in braided hammocks.

What plants and animals live in the Amazon forest?

Strange animals like the bird-eating spider, the birdwing butterfly, carnivorous ants,

poisonous frogs, and piranhas live in the Amazon forest. Even the slowest animal,

___ ___ ___ (*article*) sloth, lives there. There are also different species of plants there, some
  9

of which are very mysterious. Scientists hope that these am___z___ ___ ___ (*adjective*) plants
                10

can be used to treat serious illnesses in the future.

Excerpt from *The Temple of the Ruby of Fire*
(Originally published in Italy by Edizioni Piemme *Il tempio del rubino di fuoco*)

© 2016 Scholastic Education International (S) Pte Ltd · ISBN 978-981-4629-94-2

Why is the forest in danger?

illegal	the	its

Today, the forest is in danger. _____ (*possessive*

                  11

determiner) trees are being cut down illegally to make space for

fields. This _____ (*adjective*) logging puts the flora

            12

and fauna in _____ (*article*) Amazon forest in danger.

            13

Many species run the risk of becoming extinct, and many more

have already become extinct.

Why is the forest important?

a	the	our	ours	bad	big	yours

The Amazon plants help to keep the planet healthy. When there is too

much carbon dioxide in the atmosphere, _____ (*article*)

           14

earth gets very hot. This is _____ (*article*) phenomenon

           15

called the greenhouse effect. This greenhouse effect is _____ (*adjective*),

           16

and can have many terrible effects on us. The _____ (*adjective*) forests absorb

           17

the carbon dioxide, and help to remove much of these gases. We all need to do our part

to protect this environment of _____ (*possessive pronoun*). _____

           18   19

(*possessive determiner*) future depends on everyone's decisions, including _____

           20

(*possessive pronoun*) and mine.

**Remember, the Amazon forest is a precious treasure for everyone in
the world, and all of us must take the responsibility of saving it.**

Excerpt from *The Temple* [...]
[Originally published in Italy by Edizioni Piemme *Il tempio del rubino di fuoco*]

7 The Telltail Tavern

Both Trap and Thea had discovered something newsworthy, and were going to share their stories.

Trap began his story. "Do you remember that friend of mine I used to play pool with?" he asked. "The one with the scar on his tail and a black patch on one eye? His name is **Lefty Limburger**. Last Sunday I was playing pool with Lefty at the Telltail Tavern. Have you ever been there?"

I frowned. "I'd rather eat a piece of moldy cheese than be seen in that place!" ...

"Well, I met up with my old friend Lefty. And he told me a secret," Trap began. He lowered his voice. "You see, his niece is a friend of the mailmouse's cousin. And she lives next to the brother-in-law of one of the guards at the mouseum. Well, he told the brother-in-law, who told the mailmouse's cousin, who told Lefty's niece, who told Lefty."

"Who told who *what*?" I asked, growing *IMPATIENT*.

"Don't get your tail in a twist, Gerry," said Trap, smirking. "That's what I'm about to tell you. The mouseum guard said that the *Mona Mousa* has been taken to a lab to be **X-RAYED**. And that can only mean one thing. There is something hidden underneath the painting!"

Now it was Thea's turn. She smoothed her fur and began her story.

Simple sentences can be formed in different ways:

1. Subject + verb + object, e.g. **Trap** began **his story**.

- The **subject** is the one carrying out the action.
- The **verb** tells about the action.
- The **object** is the thing that receives the action.

2. Subject + verb + indirect object + direct object, e.g. **Trap** told **us** his story.

- The **indirect object** is the person who receives the direct object.

Excerpt from *The Mona Mousa Code*
(Originally published in Italy by Edizioni Piemme *Il sorriso di Monna Topisa*)

"Do you remember my boyfriend?" she asked. "The one with the **blue eyes** and blond fur? He always wears cheddar *cologne*...."

"You mean the one who lives in a castle and is allergic to blue cheese?" I asked.

"No, no," my sister snapped. "I got rid of that one ages ago." ...

"Well, now I have a *new* boyfriend," Thea said. "His name is Frick Tapioca, and he is the mouseum's art expert. He told me a secret. While they were restoring the *Mona Mousa*, Frick discovered that there is another painting underneath the surface. He is examining the **X-RAY** results right now!"

Chew on it!

In the sentence "He told me a secret.", identify the subject, verb, direct object, and indirect object.

A.   Circle the subject of each sentence and underline the verb.

1. Trap knew Lefty Limburger.

2. They played pool.

3. Lefty revealed a secret.

4. The mouseum guard leaked the information.

5. They found a hidden painting!

B.   Circle the direct object of each sentence.

1. Thea smoothed her fur.

2. She heard something.

3. She found a new boyfriend.

4. Frick restores paintings.

5. He discovered another painting.

© 2016 Scholastic Education International (S) Pte Ltd ISBN 978-981-4629-94-2

Excerpt from *The Mona Mousa Code*
(Originally published in Italy by Edizioni Piemme *Il sorriso di Monna Topisa*)

A. **Rearrange the words / phrases below so that the sentences make sense. Punctuate your sentences. The sentences will tell you what the group did next.**

1.   Thea   her sports car   drove

    _____

2.   ran   she   a red light

    _____

3.   the truck   almost   them   hit

    _____

    _____

4.   the place   reached   they

    _____

    _____

B. **Where do you think the group went? Look at the picture below and complete the sentences. Use the words / phrases in the box to help you.**

> held   relics   modern artwork

Frick Tapioca worked there.

1.   The ground floor housed _____ .

2.   The second floor _____ masterpieces.

3.   The third floor displayed _____

    _____ .

They went to the m_____ .

Excerpt from *The Mona Mousa Code*
(Originally published in Italy by Edizioni Piemme *Il sorriso di Monna Topisa*)   © 2016 Scholastic Education International (S) Pte Ltd ISBN 978-981-4629-94-2

Read the text below. Some of the sentences are wrong. Write the correct sentences above the wrong ones.

We went to the lab. Frick Tapioca us greeted.

Thea a question asked Frick. "What did you find, Frick?" Frick frowned. "I can't give you any information. That's top secret!"

Frick's ear Thea stroked. "There are no secrets between us now, are there?" she crooned.

Frick's fur went red. "Well …," Frick hesitated. Then he looked at Trap, Benjamin, and me. "Who are these people?" "They're family. You can trust them," said Thea.

Frick everything told us. "Last week, I started to restore the *Mona Mousa*. I scratched a fragment of paint off the canvas. noticed I a hidden painting. It was hidden underneath the *Mona Mousa*! Mousardo da Munchie created a hidden painting!"

Frick a CD us showed. "The hidden painting shows eleven objects," he said. "I them reconstructed. They're all on this disk."

He loaned the CD Thea. When we returned home, Benjamin inserted the CD into the computer. We saw the images on the screen!

Excerpt from *The Mona Mousa Code*
(Originally published in Italy by Edizioni Piemme *Il sorriso di Monna Topisa*)

8 The Pelican's Pillar

There were eleven pictures representing eleven places in New Mouse City. We had to visit each one to find the hidden letters in order to solve the mystery.

"This won't be easy," I said. "We need to visit each of the eleven places and search for a letter hidden in each one to solve the mystery. That's like searching for a needle in a stack of STRING CHEESE!"

Trap smiled confidently. "Don't get your fur in a tangle, Cousinkins." he said. "I've got friends **all over town**. You name it, and I'll tell you how to find it."

"All right, then. How about the Pelican's Pillar?" I asked. "It's somewhere in the fish market — but where?" ...

"Go to the squid stall and ask for Coral Cockle," Trap continued. "Tell her Trap sent you. She'll take you where you need to go."

Thea and I headed to the fish market together. As we approached, we heard the loud **SQUEAKS** of fish sellers. The market was packed with stalls of fishermice selling seafood. ...

I began to feel nervous. The fish seemed to be glaring at me with their creepy bulging eyes. I was so anxious that I didn't notice a nearby fish seller about to dump a bucket of seawater over his fish to keep them fresh. All of a sudden . . . SPLASH! The salty water drenched me.

"Jumping gerbil babies!" I cried. My suit was RUINED!

Thea shook her head. "**You should be more careful**," she scolded.

We use the **simple present tense** to talk about things that are happening now. We add "-s" to the end of most regular verbs when the subject is singular, e.g. Thea **shakes** her head. We do not add "-s" to the verb if the subject is plural, e.g. We **need** to visit each of the eleven places.

We use the **present continuous tense** to talk about actions that take place at the time of speaking. We use "am", "is", or "are", together with the "-ing" form of the verb, e.g. Everyone **is staring** at us.; I **am feeling** nervous.

Excerpt from *The Mona Mousa Code*
(Originally published in Italy by Edizioni Piemme *Il sorriso di Monna Topisa*)

© 2016 Scholastic Education International (S) Pte Ltd ISBN 978-981-4629-94-2

The Pelican's Pillar

"It wasn't my fault," I protested. I stepped toward Thea …

… and slipped on a fish bone! I fell **flat on my back**, knocking into a fish stall. A giant tuna fish plopped into my arms. …

By now, a crowd had gathered. They seemed to think my fish problems were funny.

"Everyone's staring at us," Thea whispered. "Oh, Gerry Berry, why do you always have to make a scene?"

 **Chew on it!**

How would Geronimo reply Thea in the present continuous tense using the verb "make"?

A. Complete the table with correct verbs in the simple present tense.

	Singular	Plural
1	asks	
2		feel
3		hear
4	keeps	
5		tell
6	visits	

B. Write the verbs in the present continuous tense.

		Singular	Plural
1	go		are going
2	dump	is/am dumping	
3	keep		
4	say		
5	search		
6	sell		

© 2016 Scholastic Education International (S) Pte Ltd ISBN 978-981-4629-94-2

Thea and Geronimo get some help from Trap's friends. Fill in each blank with the simple present tense form of the verb in brackets. Then match the clue(s) they find at each place.

Coral Cockle _____
                    1
(own) a stall at the fish

market. She _____
                    2
(lead) Geronimo, Thea,

and Benjamin to see a tall

marble column with carvings

of pelicans. Each pelican

had a fish in its beak.

Larry Licorice _____ (work) at the courthouse.
                        3
He _____ (owe) Trap a favor, so he helps
        4
Thea for free. He _____ (show) Thea a
                            5
measuring tool.

Steven Spielmouse, the film director, _____
                                              6
(use) an ancient cup. He _____ (dislike) Trap
                                  7
because Trap ruined his prop right before shooting!

Benny Bluewhiskers _____ (work) at the Cheese
                            8
Factory. After examining the cheese, if the cheese is

good, Benny _____ (sign) the
                    9
certificate, and _____ (stamp)
                        10
it with a seal. The Cheese Factory also

has a fountain that flows with cheese.

Excerpt from *The Mona Mousa Code*
(Originally published in Italy by Edizioni Piemme *Il sorriso di Monna Topisa*)

Read the text on pages 38–39 again. Complete what Geronimo must have been thinking or feeling when he went to the fish market. Use the simple present or present continuous tense of the verb in brackets.

The market is packed with stalls of fishermice selling seafood. This is the first time

I _____ (see) so many fish in one place!

1

"Thea, I _____ (feel) really nervous. The fish

2

_____ (look) at me with their creepy bulging eyes!"

3

SPLASH! As a fish seller _____ (dump) a bucket of seawater over

4

his fish, the salt water splashes on me and _____ (ruin) my suit!

5

I _____ (love) this suit and now it is gone!

6

Of course, it doesn't help that instead of helping me, Thea _____

7

(shake) her head and _____ (give) me a scolding!

8

I walk towards Thea, but I slip on a fish bone and _____ (fall) flat

9

on my back. To make matters worse, a giant tuna fish plops in my arms.

"Geronimo, what are you doing?" whispered Thea. "Everyone _____

10

(laugh) at us now."

Excerpt from The Mona Mouse Code
(Originally published in Italy by Edizioni Piemme Il sorriso di Monna Topisa)

9 The Cat's Rock

We had already found five clues. We were on our way to find the sixth. Trap had arranged a contact for us — Chuck Choptail, the owner of the roller coaster.

We arrived at the amousement park at six o'clock. The sun was setting, and the bright lights of the rides were starting to come on. We could see the big Ferris wheel, the merry-go-round, and the bumper cars. ...

We walked over to the **roller coaster**. A short mouse was sitting on a barrel of fish, counting a pile of coins. When he saw us, he muttered, "One adult and one child?"

"Mr. Chuck Choptail?" I asked. "We need some information. My cousin Trap said you might help us." ...

"Anything for a cousin of Trap's," Slick replied. "But first, how about a nice ride on the **roller coaster**?"

I gulped. "Oh, no, thank you," I said.

But Benjamin tugged on my sleeve. "Please, Uncle. It looks like fun!"

I hated to disappoint my nephew. "You can take a ride on it if you want."

SLICK frowned. "You can't let a little mouse like that go on by himself!" he scolded. He pushed us both toward a red roller coaster car. Benjamin hopped right inside. I started to back away, but Slick tripped me with his paw.

We use the **simple past tense** to talk about something that happened in the past.

For most **regular verbs**, we form the simple past tense by adding "-d", "-ed", e.g. We **arrived** at the park.; We **walked** over to the roller coaster.

Irregular verbs have special past tense forms, e.g. He **saw** us.; Oh, no, thank you, I **said**.

 Excerpt from *The Mona Mousa Code* (Originally published in Italy by Edizioni Piemme *Il sorriso di Monna Topisa*)

"Fasten your seat belts and enjoy the ride," Slick said, grinning.

"Let me out!" I screamed. But it was too late. The car had started lurching forward. I was trapped!

Chew on it!

Can you find more examples of the simple past tense in the passage?

 There are different ways to form the simple past tense. We add "–d" or "–ed" after most regular verbs. Irregular verbs have special past tense forms.

Regular verb	Simple past tense
arrive	
	hated
count	
disappoint	
	frowned
gulp	
help	
push	
start	
walk	
	hopped
	replied
	tripped
	tugged

Irregular verb	Simple past tense
are	
begin	
	broke
	fell
	went
	got
is	
	said
see	
set	
	sat
	took
	told
	woke

© 2016 Scholastic Education International (S) Pte Ltd ISBN 978-981-4629-94-2

Excerpt from *The Mona Mousa Code*
(Originally published in Italy by Edizioni Piemme *Il sorriso di Monna Topisa*)

Change all the verbs in bold to their past tense form. Draw a line through the correct list of verbs in the puzzle below to get to Cat's Rock.

"I **am** so excited, Uncle Geronimo!" yelled Benjamin.

"**Do** you want to go on the merry-go-round with me? Please **say** yes!"

"Why don't we **find** the clue first? Then you can **go** for a ride," replied Geronimo weakly. How can I **tell** him that I am afraid of such rides, and that roller coasters **make** me sick?

"Let's **look** for Chuck Choptail first, Benjamin. Do you **think** he is that mouse sitting on the barrel, counting coins?"

"Yes! That was how Uncle Trap described him. Do you think he **knows** anything about the Cat's Rock?"

"Well, let's **ask** him!"

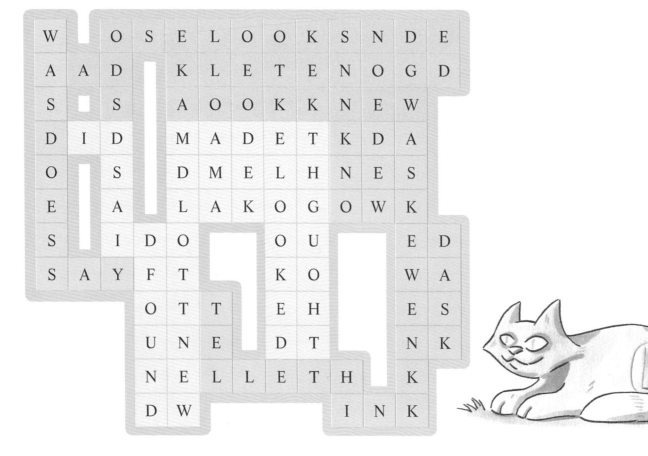

Excerpt from *The Mona Mousa Code*
(Originally published in Italy by Edizioni Piemme *Il sorriso di Monna Topisa*)

© 2016 Scholastic Education International (S) Pte Ltd ISBN 978-981-4629-94-2

Someone has been following the group in their search for clues! Complete the sentences below. Use the past tense form of the verb in brackets, and the clues in the pictures.

1 At The Fish Market

Coral Cockle told us that an old lady asked to see

the Pelican's Pillar. She wore a red head scarf with blue dots and

_____

_____ (carry).

An old lady with a basket of apples

2 AT THE COURTHOUSE

A veiled woman

Larry Licorice told Thea that a widow wanted to take a picture of

the Tail Measure. She _____

_____ (wear).

3 At the Film Studio

Thea and Geronimo saw a mouse _____

_____ (dress) in the director's

office. The mouse inspected the goblet before sneaking off.

A Roman Gladiator

4 At the Cheese Factory

Mysterious mice with floral pants and striped vests

Benny Bluewhiskers _____

_____

_____ (notice).

All of them took particular interest in the clues!

© 2016 Scholastic Education International (S) Pte Ltd ISBN 978-981-4629-94-2

THE MYSTERY PLACE

A. Geronimo wrote to his friend to tell him what had happened. Rearrange the words of some of the sentences. Then rewrite the note correctly in the space below.

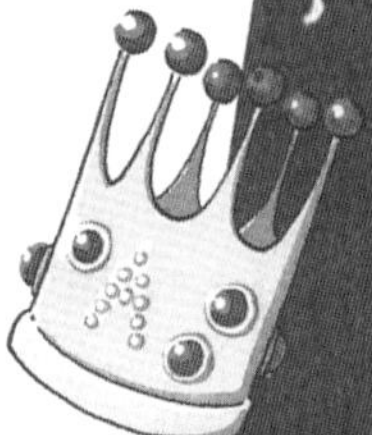

Mousardo da Munchie a mystery us left. We eleven pictures discovered. They were hidden underneath the *Mona Mousa* painting. We old encyclopedias researched. After much searching, we figured out the clues. Since then, we have been searching for the eleven letters. all the clues we found. Now, all that is left is to work out the key word. need we the final word.

_____

_____

_____

_____

_____

_____

_____

_____

_____

_____

_____

Excerpt from *The Mona Mousa Code*
Originally published in Italy by Edizioni Piemme *Il sorriso di Monna Lisa*
© 2016 Scholastic Education International (S) Pte Ltd ISBN 978-981-4629-94-2

B. Complete the paragraph below using either the present or past tense of the verbs in brackets. Also write your answers in the graphic below to find out the mystery place in the blue column.

Clues:

The one who _____ (solve) the puzzle will find the place. A long
1

time ago, this place _____ (be) a maze of many corridors. Those who
2

_____ (begin) the journey may never find their way out. Once you
3

_____ (stray), you would get lost. When the city was _____
4   5

(threaten) during the Great War of the Cats, Mousado da Munchie _____
6

(hide) it. Today, it _____ (remain) hidden, in the center of the city.
7

New Mouse City, _____ (build) over
8

the remains of Old Mouse City, covers the truth. It is

only when some brave mouse _____
9

(shout) from the highest point, that you will find it. As the

voice echoes, something wondrous will happen. Then and

only then, will you uncover the ancient library that once

_____ (stand) in the heart of town.
10

© 2016 Scholastic Education International (S) Pte Ltd ISBN 978-981-4629-94-2
Excerpt from *The Mona Mousa Code*
(Originally published in Italy by Edizioni Piemme *Il sorriso di Morina Topisa*)

Grandfather had a crazy plan to publish a guide book to Ratzikistan. He even tricked me into joining them on their trip. So here we are in Grandfather's supercamper, trying to find our way.

Now there were only four of us. Granddad, of course, sat behind the wheel. Tina **banged** pots and pans in the kitchen. My sister took pictures, leaning out the window. And I read the map. I tried to give Grandfather William directions, but as usual, he wouldn't listen. When I told him to turn left, he insisted on turning right.

"Don't be a ▓▓▓▓▓▓▓▓▓▓▓▓▓, Grandson!" he barked. "I know where we're going. You forget, I've **TRAVELED** all over the world. I have my own map right here inside the old noggin." He tapped his head. "Yep, I've got a memory like a steel trap. I can find my way to the Swiss Cheese Islands with my eyes closed. I can make it to Mouse Everest with one paw tied behind my back. I can even walk and **chew cheese** at the same time."

The right road to Ratzikistan.

In the end, we got lost.

We traveled for hours along a deserted road. We didn't pass one **SINGLE** road sign.

By nightfall, we found ourselves in the **MIDDLE** of a forest. Granddad didn't seem to mind. He just kept driving and driving.

We use **prepositions** to show the relationship between words. We use:

- **prepositions of place** (e.g. "under", "over", "inside", "beside", "in", "in front of") to show **where** something happens, e.g. Granddad sat **behind** the wheel.; Tina banged pots and pans **in** the kitchen.

- **prepositions of time** (e.g. "in", "at", "on", "by", "until", "during", "for", "since") to show **when** something happens, e.g. We traveled **for** hours.; **By** nightfall, we found ourselves in the forest.

Chew on it!

What does the phrase "in the middle of" means?

Excerpt from *A Cheese-Colored Camper*
(Originally published in Italy by Edizioni Piemme *Un camper color formaggio*)

© 2016 Scholastic Education International (S) Pte Ltd ISBN 978-981-4629-94-2

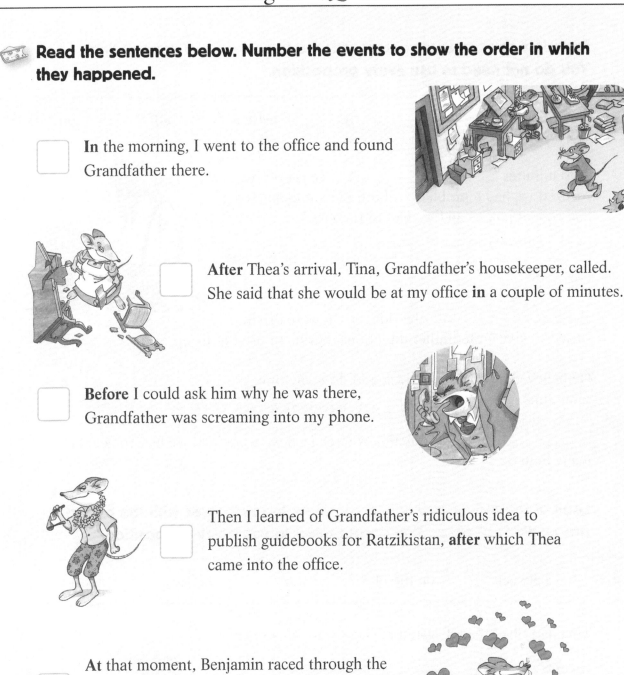

🧀 **Read the sentences below. Number the events to show the order in which they happened.**

☐ **In** the morning, I went to the office and found Grandfather there.

☐ **After** Thea's arrival, Tina, Grandfather's housekeeper, called. She said that she would be at my office **in** a couple of minutes.

☐ **Before** I could ask him why he was there, Grandfather was screaming into my phone.

☐ Then I learned of Grandfather's ridiculous idea to publish guidebooks for Ratzikistan, **after** which Thea came into the office.

☐ **At** that moment, Benjamin raced through the door and informed me that we were going to Ratzikistan! Why didn't anyone tell me?

☐ **By** the time Tina came however, I was already in a fit of rage — there was something they had not told me!

© 2016 Scholastic Education International (S) Pte Ltd ISBN 978-981-4629-94-2

A. **Complete the sentences below with the correct prepositions of time. You do not need to use every preposition.**

| at | in | during | by | before | after | on |

1. Two minutes _____ we set off, we realized we had a problem — both Benjamin and Trap had rodent pox — and we had to turn back.

2. _____, there were six of us, but now, only four.

3. _____ the ride, as we were driving, I tried to give Grandfather directions, but he refused to listen.

4. He believed he could multitask and do many things _____ the same time.

5. _____ the time we realized we were lost, we had traveled for many hours.

B. **Look at the picture below and complete the sentences with the correct prepositions of place. You do not need to use every preposition.**

| in | between | on top of | on | below | beside |

1. Tina had filled the refrigerator. There were all sorts of cheeses _____ the refrigerator.

2. The eggs were _____ the first shelf of the door. _____ the eggs was more cheese.

3. The water was placed _____ the juice. Only the jams and syrups were outside, _____ the refrigerator.

Excerpt from *A Cheese-Colored Camper*
(Originally published in Italy by Edizioni Piemme *Un camper color formaggio*)

The group realized that they were lost. Thea and Tina came up with a plan to get Geronimo to go out and ask for directions. Read their conversation below. Then complete the text using the prepositions in brackets.

Thea: Let's get Geronimo to go out and ask for directions.

Tina: We have to trick him to get out of the supercamper. First, I'll ask him to go outside to check if it is raining. Then once he is out, we can close and lock the door. That way, he'd have no choice but to make his way through the forest!

Thea: That's a brilliant plan, Tina! I can then take my shower in peace and you can cook.

By nightfall, we realized we were lost. Thea asked me to go out and look for help.

What was she thinking? I wouldn't go into the deep, dark woods alone! Thea and Tina tricked me into going out. _____ (after),

I heard SLAM! They had _____ (behind).

I knocked furiously on the door, but no one answered.

Then I heard my sister singing _____ (in).

She would probably be in there for an hour!

Tina was slamming her rolling pin

_____

(on), making her lasagna.

What was I going to do? I was _____ (in).

The branches _____ (over) terrified me.

I ran in fear as I saw shadows looming overhead.

© 2016 Scholastic Education International (S) Pte Ltd · ISBN 978-981-4629-94-2

11 Stilton Himself?

We were lost, and Thea and Tina tricked me into going out to look for help. I wandered into the forest, and could not find my way back to the camper. I ran until I met a stranger.

I told him my whole tale. About Grandfather William, the supercamper, and getting lost. …

Then I told him my name, *Geronimo Stilton*.

"Stilton!" he exclaimed. "*Geronimo Stilton*, the famouse writer? I have read all of your books!" He shook my paw, excitedly. "My name is Sylvester Squaretail," he announced. "May I have your autograph? With my name, too?"

I grinned. I must admit I love running into my fans. They're so sweet. So sincere. So smart. How do I know they're smart? They must be. They like to read my books!

I didn't have any paper, so I wrote my autograph on a leaf. …

Sylvester slipped the leaf into his pocket. I could tell he was one happy rodent.

I chewed my whiskers. I'd be happy, too, if I could find my way back to the camper. And what about Ratzikistan? Maybe Sylvester knew how to get there.

"Ratzikistan!" he exclaimed when I asked. "You're in the middle of the Fossil Forest. Ratzikistan is in the OPPOSITE direction."

We use **modal verbs** before the base form of other verbs. We use:

- "may" to give or ask for permission, or to talk about something that is likely to happen, e.g. **May** I have your autograph?; Geronimo **may** sign the autograph.

- "can" and "could" to say if someone is able to do something, e.g. I **can** tell you how to get back.; I **could** tell he was happy.

- "will" to talk about one's intention, e.g. I **will** give you directions.

- "must" to talk about necessity, e.g. I **must** admit I love the attention.

 Excerpt from *A Cheese-Colored Camper*
(Originally published in Italy by Edizioni Piemme *Un camper color formaggio*)

© 2016 Scholastic Education International (S) Pte Ltd   ISBN 978-981-4629-94-2

Cheese niblets! I knew Grandfather had been driving the wrong way. I groaned.

"Don't worry," said Sylvester. "I can tell you how to get back to your camper. Then I'll give you directions to Ratzikistan."

Chew on it!

What does "I'll" mean, who does it refer to, and what does it tell you?

 A. **Circle the correct full phrase.**

1. He'll: He will / He would

2. She'll: She will / She would

3. He'd: He will / He would

4. You'd: You will / You would

5. Won't: Will not / Would not

6. Wouldn't: Will not / Would not

7. Can't   Cannot / Could not

8. Couldn't   Cannot / Could not

9. Mustn't   Cannot / Must not

B. **Circle the correct answers.**

1. Geronimo thought he (could / may) remember all the directions, so he did not to write them down.

2. He started down the path, but after a while, he realized that he (could / must) not find his way to the camper.

3. He wondered if he (would / must) find his way back.

4. He sniffed the air and smelled lasagna. So he knew that he (will / must) be close to the camper!

5. He (couldn't / wouldn't) wait to tell his family about his adventures.

6. He thought they (can / would) be worried about him. Instead, he found them seated at the table having dinner.

Excerpt from *A Cheese-Colored Camper*
(Originally published in Italy by Edizioni Piemme *Un camper color formaggio*)

Fill in each blank with the correct modal verb to suit the situation. Some modal verbs may be used more than once.

can	could	would	may	must	will

1. We knew that we had finally reached Ratzikistan as we _____ see a road sign through the fog.

2. "I did it! I told you I could find the way. I _____ find my way to anywhere!" said Grandfather.

3. Tina declared, "We _____ find a supermarket. We do not have any food left!"

4. Geronimo thought they _____ not be able to find a supermarket in Ratzikistan, but Tina found one!

5. "_____ I have five pounds of cheddar, six jars of sardines, and three loaves of bread?" Tina asked the shop assistant.

6. "_____ I suggest we find somewhere else, Tina?" I whispered. "I don't think you _____ be able to get what you want from this dingy shop."

7. Tina insisted, "Don't worry. I _____ make sure they get me everything I need." A few minutes later, Tina got what she wanted!

Excerpt from *A Cheese-Colored Camper*
(Originally published in Italy by Edizioni Piemme *Un camper color formaggio*)

© 2016 Scholastic Education International (S) Pte Ltd ISBN 978-981-4629-94-2

A. **Complete each sentence below with the modal verb and verb in brackets.**

1. "_____ (can't, give) me proper directions, Geronimo?" yelled Grandfather. "I'm trying," replied Geronimo. "Try harder!" screamed Grandfather.

2. "_____ (will, find) Ratzikistan," said Grandfather confidently.

3. "Tina, _____ (may, have) more lasagna?" asked Grandfather.

4. "No, it is not good for your health. _____ (must, watch) your diet!" ordered Tina.

B. **Write a sentence or question for each situation below. Use the most suitable modal verb.**

1. Show how brave Thea is from the activities she is able to do, such as parachuting and racing on her motorcycle.

   Thea _____

   _____

   _____

2. Tina wants to ask Geronimo to help her find the things in her shopping list.

   "_____

   _____

   _____?" asked Tina.

We had reached Ratzikistan. We finally got to a clearing. I decided to take a walk and stretch my paws a little.

I took a few steps, but I didn't get far. Seconds later, Tina's whistle practically pierced my eardrums. She uses it to signal that dinner is ready.

"Come on, shake a paw!" she called. "You don't want your food to get cold!"

We sat down at the table. Tina was busy dishing up the meal. She placed one OLIVE and a piece of lettuce on Grandfather William's plate. Recently, she had decided he needed to go back on his diet.

Granddad stared at his plate and sighed.

"No complaining," Tina scolded. "You need to drop those pounds or we'll have to roll you home!"

Then she turned her attention to me. Uh-oh. Tina had other plans for me. Recently, she had decided that I was too thin. She began piling my plate high with food. I watched in horror as she filled an enormouse bowl to the brim with spaghetti. Then she slapped down plate after plate of pies, casseroles, puddings, breads, and more. There was no way I could eat all of that food. It was enough for ten mice, not one!

I felt sick. "Um, but, Tina," I began. "I have a weak stomach. I don't think —"

We use **connectors** to link words. We use:

- "and" to link ideas or things that are similar, e.g. She placed one olive **and** a piece of lettuce on the plate.

- "but" to link opposite ideas, e.g. She spoke firmly, **but** politely.

- "or" to talk about choices, e.g. I could have pies **or** casseroles.

We also use the connectors, "and", "but", or "or" to join two sentences, e.g. I took a few steps. I didn't get far.
→ I took a few steps, **but** I didn't get far.

 Excerpt from *A Cheese-Colored Camper* (Originally published in Italy by Edizioni Piemme *Un camper color formaggio*)

 ISBN 978-981-4629-94-2

A Cast-iron  Stomach

"NONSENSE!" Tina interrupted me. "I'll fix that stomach of yours. You just need to fill it with a ton of food. Soon you'll be able to eat stones!"

I CRINGED. But I didn't tell Tina I wasn't interested in eating stones. I didn't want her to hit the roof.

Meanwhile, Grandfather was eyeing my *food* with envy. He tried to steal a roll, but Tina slapped his paw away.

"I'm doing this for your own good!" she told Granddad. "As for you, *Mr.* Geronimo, you need to try harder!"

I opened my mouth to complain. Bad idea. Tina picked up a spoon and STUFFED my mouth *full of lard*.

Chew on it!

Tina scolded Granddad. She also scolded Geronimo. Which connector would you use to form a sentence from the above two sentences?

Circle the most suitable connector to use in each sentence.

1. Tina decided on the eating plan for both Grandfather (and / or) Geronimo.

2. Grandfather was getting fat (and / but) unhealthy.

3. She stuffed Geronimo with spaghetti (and / or) pies.

4. Tina was strict, (or / but) caring, so Grandfather listened to her.

5. All Grandfather wanted was one more roll (but / or) pie, but Tina refused to let him have it.

6. When Tina stuffed his face with lard, Geronimo wondered if lard (and / or) glue tasted worse!

© 2016 Scholastic Education International (S) Pte Ltd ISBN 978-981-4629-94-2

Excerpt from *A Cheese-Colored Camper*
(Originally published in Italy by Edizioni Piemme *Un campeggio color formaggio*)

Complete the following text with "and", "but", or "or".

A.   Instructions from Tina to Grandfather:

1.   You can only have one dish. You can have either lasagna

_____ spaghetti.

2.   You must eat more of both vegetables

_____ fruit, and stop eating

so much dessert.

3.   You can have some cheese, _____

not too much.

4.   If you want more, you must ask me, _____ not steal

from Geronimo's plate.

B.   Instructions from Tina to Geronimo:

1.   You must eat more _____ strengthen your stomach.

2.   You can choose to eat less, _____ you must eat at

least two bowls of spaghetti.

3.   You must also drink a lot of milk, _____ water, if we

cannot get milk.

4.   You must not give your Grandfather any food, _____

you cannot let him steal your food.

Excerpt from *A Cheese-Colored Camper*
(Originally published in Italy by Edizioni Piemme *Un camper color formaggio*)

© 2016 Scholastic Education International (S) Pte Ltd ISBN 978-981-4629-94-2

A Cast-iron Stomach

Using a connector, combine each pair of sentences into one sentence. An example is provided below.

Tina likes cooking. She is a great cook.
Tina likes cooking <u>and</u> she is a great cook.

1. Most people feared Grandfather. Tina was not afraid of him.

   _____

   _____

2. Geronimo did not want to go to Ratzikistan. He threw a big fit in the office.

   _____

   _____

3. Grandfather told Geronimo that he could break his heart. Grandfather also told him that he could choose to join them on the trip.

   _____

   _____

4. Grandfather was sneaky. He tricked Geronimo into going with them.

   _____

   _____

5. Geronimo did not want to go. He went in the end.

   _____

   _____

Excerpt from *A Cheese-Colored Camper*
(Originally published in Italy by Edizioni Piemme *Un camper color formaggio*)

A Road Trip to Ratzikistan

A. Look at the picture of Grandfather's supercamper below. Write three sentences using prepositions of place to describe the supercamper. Also, write three sentences using prepositions of time to talk about what Grandfather would do in the supercamper.

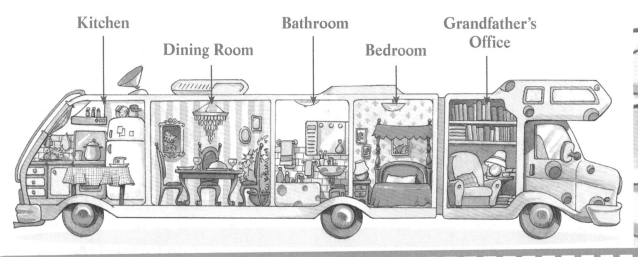

Kitchen Dining Room Bathroom Bedroom Grandfather's Office

Description of the supercamper (using prepositions of place):

1. _____

_____

2. _____

_____

3. _____

_____

What Grandfather would do in the supercamper (using prepositions of time):

4. _____

_____

5. _____

_____

6 _____

_____

Excerpt from *A Cheese-Colored Camper*
(Originally published in Italy by Edizioni Piemme *Un camper color formaggio*)

B. **Complete the description of Ratzikistan using the words in the box. Some words may be used more than once.**

and	but	or	will	can	must

Ratzikistan landscape:

It is a land of icy mountains and snow-covered valleys.

It is freezing, _____ it is worth the trip up;
                          1
the air is very fresh. The landscape is breathtaking.

Things to do:

1.   Choose one. You _____ go sledding down steep slopes
                                    2
     and over frozen lakes, _____ you can zip around in
                                          3
     a snowmobile.

2.   Try out the local sports:

     A. Make your own snowballs, _____ take part
                                               4
         in the snowball fight with the locals!

     B. If you enjoy fishing, you _____
                                               5
         not miss the stinking fish contest!
         You guessed it, the stinkiest one wins!

     C. You _____ learn about how the
                     6
         people in Ratzikistan live by learning to build an igloo.

3.   If you love cheese, you _____ love the cheddarella
                                        7
     cheese. One taste is all you need to get hooked!

© 2016 Scholastic Education International (S) Pte Ltd ISBN 978-981-4629-94-2

Excerpt from *A Cheese-Colored Camper*
(Originally published in Italy by Edizioni Piemme *Un camper color formaggio*)

Answers

Unit 1
Pages 6–7
Chew on it! question:
office; clock; minutes; tone; mouse; block; shower, teeth; time; station; train; sound; crowd; stairs; cat; subway; exit; work; sandwich; tail; pulp; lady

Page 7
A. Proper nouns: Geronimo Stilton; *The Rodent's Gazette*; Mouse Island; Uncle Geronimo
Common nouns: uncle, newspaper; station; cat; rodents; hero; mice; stairs
Cross out: All; safety; terrified; fact; scared

B.
1. train: C
2. The Press Club: P
3. Geronimo: P
4. sandwich: C
5. telephone: C
6. Benjamin: P
7. names: C
8. Ratoff Castle: P

Page 8
1. Gazette
2. Thea
3. X
4. motorcycle
5. door
6. office
7. X
8. subway
9. information
10. Monday
11. rodents
12. signs

Page 9
1. station
2. sound
3. cat
4. subway
5. exit
6. mouse
7. stairs

Unit 2
Pages 10–11
Chew on it! question:
The pronoun would be "It".

Page 11
1. She
2. They
3. They
4. She
5. He
6. it
7. He

Page 12
1. She
2. him
3. he
4. him
5. he
6. I
7. We
8. you
9. us
10. I
11. she
12. they

Page 13
A. 1. Trap wanted money for the information.
   He threatened to sell it to Sally Ratmousen.
   2. Trap knew that Sally is Geronimo's archrival.
   He tried to persuade her to pay for the latest scoop.
   3. Thea and Geronimo were really angry with Trap.
   They could not believe they were related to him.

B:
Trap	Geronimo
I: Trap	you: Trap
me: Trap	You: Trap

Trap	Thea
you: Geronimo	we: Trap, Thea and Geronimo
I: Trap	(or Trap and Thea)
you: Geronimo	us: Thea and Geronimo

Unit 3
Pages 14–15
Chew on it! question:
Action verbs: stopped; look out; get by; organizes; put up; grinned; divide; twirled; stuck out; shook
Saying verbs: began; tells; finished; squeaked; said; told

Page 15
1. heard
2. marched
3. ordered; freeze
4. turned; look
5. told
6. suggested; share
7. complained
8. said
9. felt
10. agreed

Page 16
1. tell
2. examine; think
3. find
4. gives
5. made

Page 17
A. 1. tell; knows
   2. find; know; get
   3. organize; buy
   4. pay
B. Accept all reasonable answers.

Activity 1
Pages 18–19
A.
1. them (Pinky, Geronimo, Trap, and Thea)
2. She (Pinky)
3. them (police)
4. you (Pinky)
5. it (map)
6. He (Goofsnout P. Goofus)
7. I (Geronimo)
8. him (Geronimo)
9. They (Trap and Geronimo)
10. she (Thea)

B.
1. Remove
2. Climb
3. Walk
4. reach; cross; throw; hang
5. Make; stay

C. Sally Ratmousen

Unit 4
Page 20
Chew on it! question:
Adjectives to describe the plants and animals in the Amazon: lush; green; multicolored; enormouse; hairy

Page 21
A. Circle: tired; sweaty; relaxing; aching; blistered; tiny; warm; friendly; simple; respectful; strange; same; shocked; best; obnoxious; shut

B. Fish: small; scary; colorful
Geronimo: frightened; nervous; shocked

Page 22
1. ferocious
2. sharp
3. shady
4. enormous
5. poisonous
6. long
7. impressed
8. surprised

Page 23
Accept all reasonable answers. Suggested answers:
1. This rodent is chubby and has slick black fur. He wears a huge gold medal, a thick gold watch, and a glittering diamond. He is nasty.
2. This rodent is thin and has a crooked snout. He wears a black shirt and has an evil expression.
3. This rodent is fierce, strong, enormous, muscular, and has thick brown fur.

Unit 5
Page 24
Chew on it! question:
Strongfur was referring to monkeys in general, and not to a specific monkey.

Page 25
A. Circle all the "a" (5) and "an" (1) in the passage.
B.
1. a
2. a; a
3. an

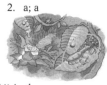

C. Circle all the "the" (4) in the passage.

Page 26
1. a
2. the; the
3. a; the
4. the
5. X; The; X
6. the; the; X
7. the
8. an

Page 27
A. 1. We waited for an hour, till after Nastytail and his crew were sound asleep.
   2. Then we headed for the Temple of the Ruby of Fire.
   3. Monkeyfur led the way inside. The light from the flickering candles cast eerie shadows all around.
   4. Monkeyfur showed us the sacrificial altar, and drawings of many different animals and plants. Then she pointed out the location of the ruby! It was right in the center.
   5. All of a sudden, we heard a bloodcurdling scream.
   6. "Do not worry. The screams are from the Howling Spirits," Monkeyfur explained.
   7. Just as I thought I would pass out, I saw a whole bunch of monkeys coming to greet Monkeyfur.
   8. She spoke to them in a strange language before showing us the main room.

62

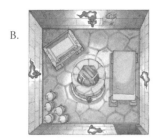

B.

Unit 6
Pages 28–29
Chew on it! question:
The professor was talking about Nastytail, Miceson, and Bones.

A. 1. their   2. their   3. his   4. our   5. his

B. theirs; ours; ours; yours

Page 30
1. our   2. ours   3. My
4. your; yours   5. your; your   6. our; our; their; his

Page 31
1. his   2. their   3. his   4. ours
5. their   6. her   7. his   8. your

Activity 2
Pages 32–33
1. large   2. dense   3. hot   4. The   5. the
6. their   7. good   8. Their   9. the   10. amazing
11. Its   12. illegal   13. the   14. the   15. a
16. bad   17. big   18. ours   19. Our   20. yours

Unit 7
Pages 34–35
Chew on it! question:
He (subject) told (verb) me (indirect object) a secret (direct object).

Pages 35
A. 1. (Trap) knew Lefty Limburger.
   2. (They) played pool.
   3. (Lefty) revealed a secret.
   4. (The mouseum guard) leaked the information.
   5. (They) found a hidden painting!

B. 1. Thea smoothed (her fur).
   2. She heard (something).
   3. She found (a new boyfriend).
   4. Frick restores (paintings).
   5. He discovered (another painting).

Page 36
A. 1. Thea drove her sports car.
   2. She ran a red light.
   3. The truck almost hit them.
   4. They reached the place.

B. 1. relics
   2. held
   3. modern artwork
   They went to the museum.

Page 37
We went to the lab. **Frick Tapioca greeted us.**
Thea asked Frick a question. "What did you find, Frick?" Frick frowned. "I can't give you any information. That's top secret!"
Thea stroked Frick's ear. "There are no secrets between us now, are there?" she crooned.
Frick's fur went red. "Well …," Frick hesitated. Then he looked at Trap, Benjamin, and me. "Who are these people?" "They're family. You can trust them," said Thea.
Frick told us everything. "Last week, I started to restore the *Mona Mousa*. I scratched a fragment of paint off the canvas. **I noticed a hidden painting.** It was hidden underneath the *Mona Mousa*!

Mousardo da Munchie created a hidden painting!"
Frick showed us a CD. "The hidden painting shows eleven objects," he said. "**I reconstructed them.** They're all on this disk."
He loaned Thea the CD. When we returned home, Benjamin inserted the CD into the computer. We saw the images on the screen!

Unit 8
Pages 38–39
Chew on it! question:
Accept all reasonable answers. Suggested answer: "I am not making a scene!"

Pages 39
A.

	Singular	Plural
1.	asks	**ask**
2.	**feels**	feel
3.	**hears**	hear
4.	keeps	**keep**
5.	**tells**	tell
6.	visits	**visit**

B.

	Singular	Plural
1.	go	**is/am going**	are going
2.	dump	is/am dumping	**are dumping**
3.	keep	**is/am keeping**	**are keeping**
4.	say	**is/am saying**	are saying
5.	search	**is/am searching**	**are searching**
6.	sell	**is/am selling**	**are selling**

Page 40
1. owns   2. leads   3. works   4. owes   5. shows
6. uses   7. dislikes   8. works   9. signs   10. stamps

paragraph 1   paragraph 3

paragraph 2   paragraph 4

Page 41
1. see / am seeing   2. feel /am feeling   3. are looking
4. is dumping/dumps   5. ruins   6. love
7. shakes   8. gives   9. fall   10. is laughing

Unit 9
Pages 42–43
Chew on it! question:
muttered; replied; gulped; tugged; hated; frowned; scolded; pushed; hopped; started; tripped; screamed; was; trapped

Pages 43

Regular verb	Simple past tense		Irregular verb	Simple past tense
arrive	**arrived**		are	**were**
hate	hated		begin	**began**
count	**counted**		**break**	broke
disappoint	**disappointed**		**fall**	fell
frown	frowned		**go**	went
gulp	**gulped**		**get**	got
help	**helped**		is	**was**
push	**pushed**		**say**	said
start	**started**		see	**saw**
walk	**walked**		set	**set**
hop	hopped		**sit**	sat
reply	replied		take	took
trip	tripped		**tell**	told
tug	tugged		**wake**	woke

Page 44
am — was
Do — Did
say — said
find — found
go — went
tell — told
make — made
look — looked
think — thought
knows — knew
ask — asked

Page 45

Accept all reasonable answers. Suggested answers:
1. She wore a red head scarf with blue dots and <u>carried a basket of apples.</u>
2. She <u>wore a veil and carried a small purple bag.</u>
3. Thea and Geronimo saw a mouse <u>dressed like a Roman gladiator</u> in the director's office.
4. Benny Bluewhiskers <u>noticed one mouse who was wearing a pair of floral pants and another in a striped vest.</u>

Activity 3
Pages 46–47

A. Mousardo da Munchie left us a mystery. We discovered eleven pictures. They were hidden underneath the *Mona Mousa* painting. We researched old encyclopedias. After much searching, we figured out the clues. Since then, we have been searching for the eleven letters. We found all the clues. Now, all that is left is to work out the key word. We need the final word.

B.
```
1 s o l v e s
  2 w a s
    3 b e g i n
4 s t r a y
    5 t h r e a t e n e d
      6 h i d
7 r e m a i n s
8 b u i l t
      9 s h o u t s
      10 s t o o d
```

Unit 10
Page 48

Chew on it! question:
The phrase means "in the center of" or "in between".

Page 49

1, 4, 2, 3, 6, 5

Page 50

A. 1. after   2. Before   3. During   4. at   5. By
B. 1. in   2. on; Below   3. beside; on top of

Page 51

Accept all reasonable answers. Suggested answers:
1. After I got out of the supercamper
2. closed and locked the door behind me
3. in the shower
4. on the kitchen table
5. in the forest alone
6. hanging over me

Unit 11
Pages 52–53

Chew on it! question:
"I'll" means "I will", it refers to Sylvester, and it tells me about Sylvester's intention to give Geronimo directions to Ratzikistan.

Page 53

A. 1. He will   2. She will   3. He would
   4. You would   5. Will not   6. Would not
   7. Cannot   8. Could not   9. Must not

B. 1. could   2. could   3. would
   4. must   5. couldn't   6. would

Page 54

1. could   2. can   3. must   4. would
5. May   6. May; will   7. will

Page 55

A. Accept all reasonable answers. Suggested answers:
   1. Why can't you give
   2. We/I will find
   3. may I have
   4. You must watch

B. Accept all reasonable answers. Suggested answers:
   1. Thea will not be afraid to parachute or race on her motorcycle.
   2. "Geronimo, can you help me find the things in my shopping list?" asked Tina.

Unit 12
Pages 56–57

Chew on it! question:
The connector would be "and". Tina scolded Granddad <u>and</u> Geronimo.

1. and   2. and   3. and
4. but   5. or   6. or

Page 58

A. 1. or   2. and   3. but   4. and
B. 1. and   2. but   3. or   4. and

Page 59

1. Most people feared Grandfather, but Tina was not afraid of him.
2. Geronimo did not want to go to Ratzikistan, and he threw a big fit in the office.
3. Grandfather told Geronimo that he could break his heart, or he could choose to join them on the trip.
4. Grandfather was sneaky, and he tricked Geronimo into going with them.
5. Geronimo did not want to go, but he went in the end.

Activity 4
Pages 60–61

A. Accept all reasonable answers.

B. 1. but   2. can   3. or   4. and
   5. must   6. can   7. will

© 2016 Scholastic Education International (S) Pte Ltd ISBN 978-981-4629-94-2